Don't Forget Us!

I · COME · FROM
KURDISTAN

Anita Ganeri

A Watts Book
LONDON · NEW YORK · SYDNEY

© Aladdin Books Ltd 1995
Designed and produced by
Aladdin Books Ltd
28 Percy Street
London W1P 9FF

First published in
Great Britain in 1995 by
Watts Books
96 Leonard Street
London EC2A 4RH

Editor: Jim Pipe
Designer: Tess Barwick
Illustrator: David Burroughs
Consultant: Andrew Penny
Photo
Research: Brooks Krikler
               Research

Printed in Belgium
All rights reserved

A CIP catalogue record for this
book is available from the
British Library.

ISBN 0 7496 2108 7

CONTENTS

INTRODUCTION

My name is Berivan and I am a Kurd. My name means "milkmaid" in the Kurdish language. Kurdistan isn't a recognised country – it is split between several different countries. The part of Kurdistan I come from is in southeastern Turkey. The Kurdish people want to have their own country and this is causing lots of problems. My family and I left our home to escape from the fighting and killing.

I often think about my friends who are still in Kurdistan. So let me tell you about my old home, my friends and family and how we used to live.

There are about 20-25 million Kurds. About a quarter live outside Kurdistan, in countries such as Germany, Great Britain and the United States. Many have been forced to leave their homes and move to other parts of Kurdistan for safety. At the end of the Gulf War in 1991, some two million Kurds fled from Iraq to Iran and Turkey to escape from attacks by the Iraqi government.

KURDISTAN TODAY

Kurdistan is the name given to a region in southwest Asia, on the borders of Turkey (right), Syria, Iran and Iraq. It is the homeland of my people, the Kurds. It covers an area of about 600,000 sq km, about the size of France.

The countries in which the Kurds live do not want them to have their own country. They treat the Kurds cruelly and do not allow them to keep their culture or identity. In Turkey, for example, we are not allowed to wear Kurdish clothes or to listen to Kurdish music. We all speak a language called Kurdish, but because we are so widely scattered, there are many different dialects. This makes it difficult for one group of Kurds to understand another.

Silav

سڵاو

(Left) The Kurdish word for 'Hello'. In Turkey and Syria, Kurdish is written in the Roman alphabet (above). In Iraq and Iran the Arabic alphabet is used (below). Armenian Kurds use the Cyrillic alphabet, which is also used for Russian.

COUNTRY AND CLIMATE

Kurdistan is a largely mountainous area. In winter, the weather in the mountains becomes bitterly cold and remote villages may be cut off by snow for up to six months of the year. The Kurds live mainly in the mountains: there is even an old Kurdish proverb which says, "The Kurds have no friends but the mountains". Others live in villages in the valleys and plains, or in cities such as Istanbul in Turkey.

Two great rivers, the Tigris and the Euphrates, rise in the mountains of Turkish Kurdistan and then flow through Iraq and Syria. They provide plenty of water for irrigation and for hydro-electric power.

(Left) Long ago, the mountain slopes were covered in great forests of oak and cedar trees. These are long gone, although some plants still thrive on the rocky mountain slopes.

Mount Ararat, the final resting place of Noah's ark in the Bible story, lies in the east of Kurdistan near the border with Armenia (see map, right).

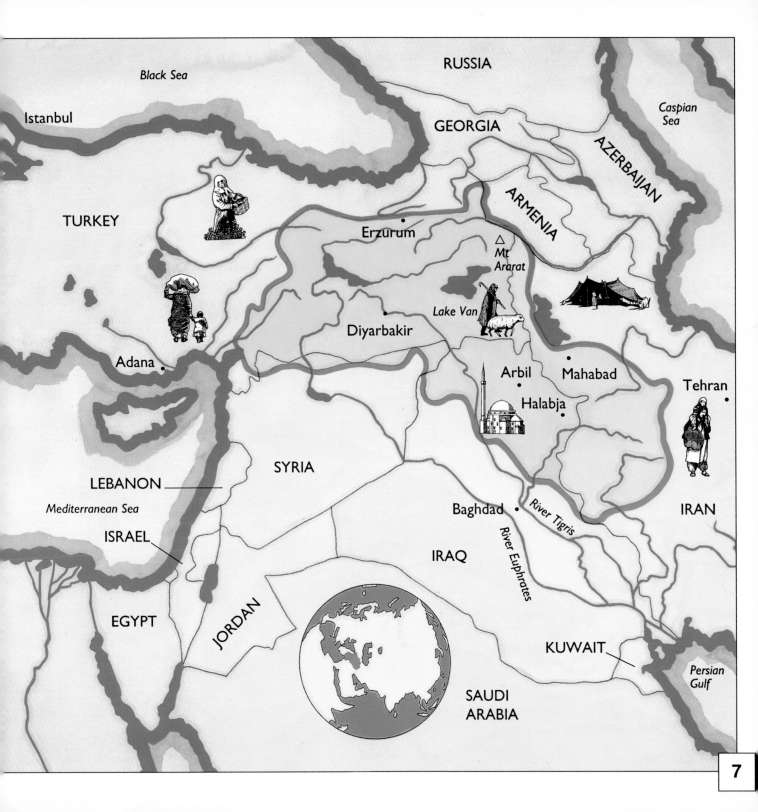

RUSSIA

Black Sea

Istanbul

GEORGIA

Caspian Sea

AZERBAIJAN

ARMENIA

TURKEY

Erzurum

Mt Ararat

Lake Van

Diyarbakir

Arbil

Mahabad

Adana

Halabja

Tehran

SYRIA

IRAN

LEBANON

Mediterranean Sea

Baghdad

River Tigris

ISRAEL

River Euphrates

IRAQ

EGYPT

JORDAN

KUWAIT

Persian Gulf

SAUDI ARABIA

Though poor, many Kurds still wear their beautifully-made traditional clothes. Men wear a patterned headscarf (left), while girls' and women's clothing (below) is often finely-woven with golden thread.

KURDISH PEOPLE

The Kurds are not related to the people of the various countries they live in. They are an ancient people, thought to be descended from a people called the Medes. The Medes conquered the area now known as Kurdistan in the 8th century BC. In turn, they were conquered by the Persians.

In the 7th century AD, the Arabs invaded the region, bringing the religion of Islam with them. Most of the Kurds converted to Islam. In return, they were allowed to keep their own lands. In the 16th century, Kurdistan became part of the Turkish Ottoman Empire. This empire broke up at the end of World War I. In 1920, the Treaty of Sevres agreed to set up an independent Kurdistan, but it was never honoured by the European powers that signed it. So the Kurds remained without a country of their own.

The Kurds have always been proud, fierce warriors. One of the great Kurdish heroes is Saladin, born in 1138 AD. During the Crusades, Saladin led the Saracen (Muslim) forces to victory over the Christians. Later he became king of Egypt and Syria. Many of his soldiers were Kurds, famous for their bravery.

THE KURDS OF TURKEY

About half of all the Kurds live in southeast Turkey. Many live in Turkish towns and cities such as Istanbul, Izmir, Adana and Mersin and have adapted to Turkish life. But, for most Kurds, life is very hard indeed. We are not allowed to learn Kurdish at school or wear Kurdish dress. In fact, the Turkish government does not even recognise us as a separate people. Instead, we are officially known as "mountain Turks".

For many years, there has been fierce fighting between the Turkish army and the PKK, or Kurdistan Workers' Party which wants freedom for the Kurdish people. In the struggle between the two sides, hundreds of Kurdish villages have been burnt down and hundreds of thousands of villagers tortured, killed or forced to flee to cities such as Diyarbakir. Not all the Kurds in Turkey support the PKK, but they all share the hope of a better life.

(Left) A Kurdish boy trying to make a living by shining shoes in the street. Shoeshine stalls are a common sight in Turkish towns and cities.

(Left) Refugees fled to Turkey in 1991 to escape Iraqi troops. Now, many are returning to northern Iraq due to Turkish attacks.

(Below) A Kurdish bakery in Turkey with traditional breads on display.

(Right) Many Kurds who fled from Iraqi troops ended up in refugee camps in Iran. Life in these camps is very hard indeed.

(Below) *Peshmergas* are Kurdish freedom fighters who hide out in the mountains. Women train and fight with the men.

KURDS IN IRAN & IRAQ

There are about six million Kurds living in Iran and about four million in Iraq. The Iranian Kurds are expected to follow the strict Islamic law of the country and to think of themselves as Iranian citizens. The Iraqi Kurds have had an even tougher time.

During the Iran-Iraq War (1980-1989) many Iraqi Kurds sided with the Iranians in protest at their treatment in Iraq. In return, the Iraqi government attacked Kurdish villages with poison gas, killing thousands of people. After the Gulf War (1990-1991), the Iraqi Kurds rebelled against Saddam Hussein and many were forced to flee for their lives to Iran and Turkey. Today, Kurds govern their own zone in northern Iraq. This is patrolled by United Nations troops.

A baby's cot made from old pallets (right). The refugees have few possessions. If they need something, they have to make it from scrap.

OUR BELIEFS

Like most Kurdish people, my family are Muslims. We believe in Allah (God) and in the teachings of Muhammed, his prophet. We turn to face Mecca, Muhammed's birthplace in Saudi Arabia, when we pray. As Muslims, we worship in buildings called mosques (see right, bottom of page). We read the Koran, our holy book, which contains the words Allah passed down to Muhammed. In Iran, Muslim women have to wear chador, a black cloth which covers their hair and clothes as a sign of modesty (see picture opposite).

Many Kurds also belong to religious groups called Sufi brotherhoods which meet to pray, sing and dance. These brotherhoods are very important in the life of Kurdish villages. Some Kurds are Yezidis. They belong to a sect called the Cult of Angels and worship an angel called *Malak Tawus* (the Peacock Angel).

This picture of the Christian Saint George (left) comes from an Assyrian Church in Arbil, Iraq. Some Kurds are Christians. Their ancestors probably converted to Christianity before the arrival of Islam in the 7th century AD.

The Yezidis' holiest shrine is at Lalesh in Iraq. Yezidis from other parts of Kurdistan sometimes make pilgrimages to this shrine.

(Below) The Great Mosque at Diyarbakir. Diyarbakir, the largest Kurdish city in Turkey, is often considered the unofficial capital of Kurdistan.

NOMADS AND TRIBES

Traditionally, the mountain Kurds lived a nomadic life, wandering from place to place in search of grazing for their herds of goats and flocks of sheep. Others lived in settled villages in the valleys. Today, though most Kurds live in towns and villages, some are still semi-nomadic. The nomads take their flocks to the high pastures for three months in the heat of the summer (see left), then bring them down to the towns to sell the animals at market. They also trade wool, leather and cheese.

Many Kurds belong to a tribe and have very strong links with other members of their tribe. Kurdish families are often very large. Parents rely on their children to care for them in their old age.

A nomad tent (right). Tents are easy to carry from place to place and to put up and take down.

FOOD AND CLOTHES

Today, many Kurds wear the dress of the country they live in. But some people, especially in more remote places, still wear traditional Kurdish dress. Women wear brightly coloured and patterned skirts and blouses, with scarves around their heads (top right). Men wear baggy trousers, shirts, sashes, waistcoats, and hats.

Traditional Kurdish food includes flat bread baked in a clay oven (bottom right), rice, and stuffed peppers and vine leaves. We also eat *kooba* – minced meat and bulgur wheat made into balls and boiled or fried. Another speciality is *sheikh mahshi* – aubergines stuffed with nuts, minced meat and spices. We make many different types of cheese from goat's or sheep's milk. We like to drink tea flavoured with cardamom spice.

This Kurdish woman is making butter using a traditional butter churn made of skins tied together and hung from a wooden frame. The churn can be carried up into the mountains in summer when there is good grazing to fatten sheep and goats and plenty of milk for butter making.

(Above) Traditional Kurdish dress.

(Below) Rhubarb is a popular Kurdish food and is usually eaten raw with salt.

RURAL AND CITY LIFE

Many young Kurds are moving into towns and cities in search of work. In the towns, they do all sorts of jobs from being shopkeepers to being mechanics and plumbers. The most important cities in Kurdistan are Mahabad in Iran, Arbil in Iraq and Diyarbakir in Turkey.

In the villages, the day begins early. The women milk the sheep and goats, then the children take them to the pastures to graze. They bring them back in the evening to be milked again. On warm summer evenings, the family sits on the flat roof of their house. They also sleep there in the hot weather.

Children may go to the local school where they have lessons in Arabic or Turkish, even though they speak Kurdish at home. This makes it very difficult for them to learn. Many Kurdish children leave school at an early age. Others never go but work with their parents.

(Right) Kurdish families collect water from the only waterhole in the town of Khalidiza in Turkey.

(Above) A Kurdish child living in the mountains being taught in an open-air school.

(Below) A barber shop in Zakho. Many Kurdish houses in Iraq have been damaged or destroyed by Iraqi troops.

WORK AND PLAY

In the mountains, the Kurds earn their living as goat and sheep herders. In the villages lower down they farm small plots of land, growing crops such as wheat, barley, lentils and different types of fruit and vegetables. Cotton and tobacco are also grown and taken to market to be sold.

Men, women and often children share the work. Kurdish women spin and weave cloth, and make rugs and carpets to sell. People do not have much spare time but they like to play a game like hockey but with a wooden ball. Many Kurds have left Turkey to live and work in Germany. They try to send money back to their families in Kurdistan.

Kurdish men like to meet up in a teahouse to drink tea and play chess or backgammon. They may also listen to tapes of Kurdish music, although it is officially banned in Turkey.

CUSTOMS AND TRADITIONS

Many of our Kurdish customs and traditions are thousands of years old. We love listening to songs or stories about Kurdish heroes. One old Kurdish story tells of Mem, a boy abandoned by his mother as a baby and brought up by a rich man called Al Pasha, and a beautiful girl called Zin. Three doves from paradise arrange for Mem and Zin to meet and fall in love. The story has a tragic ending when Mem's wicked uncle Beko tries to stop them getting married.

One of our biggest festivals is *Newroz*, the Kurdish New Year and the first day of spring. We celebrate Newroz on 21 March by lighting bonfires to mark the defeat of the evil tyrant, Dehak, by the blacksmith, Kawa, in 612 BC.

(Left) Special occasions are celebrated with feasting, singing and dancing. Dancers wear brightly coloured traditional costumes.

(Right) Kurdish stories are usually passed down by word of mouth, not written down. As she spins wool by hand, this woman tells a story to entertain her fellow workers.

WHY I'M HERE

In 1923, a treaty was signed which split Kurdish lands between the countries of Turkey, Syria, Iraq and Iran. The Kurds were left with nothing. This was the start of the struggle for freedom which continues today. We need to save our Kurdish culture and identity before it is too late.

At the end of the Gulf War in 1991, millions of Iraqi Kurds fled from Saddam Hussein's cruel government (right). The United Nations created 'safe havens' for them in northern Iraq and western countries sent food, tents and medical supplies. But thousands died from hunger and cold as they crossed the mountains. Many others have been killed or wounded in the fighting in Iraq and Turkey. This is why my family left Kurdistan. It was just too dangerous for us to stay.

Experts are still at work clearing Kurdish border villages of mines left after the 1980-1990 Iran-Iraq war.

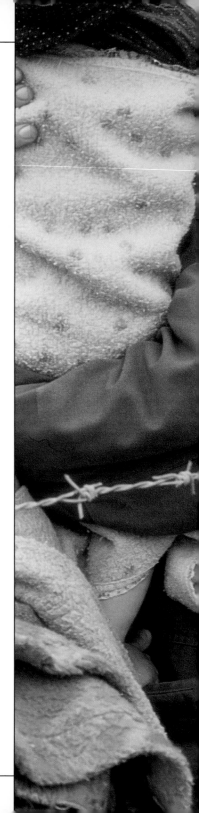

26

(Above) A mother comforts her child injured by a mine in northern Iraq.

(Below) Kurdish children earn money by hunting for scrap metal left over from the Iran-Iraq War. This can be very dangerous as some shells remain unexploded.

MY FUTURE

In 1992, elections were held in Iraqi Kurdistan and a Kurdish parliament set up in Arbil. But fighting between the rival Kurdish groups and the threat of Turkish, Iraqi and Iranian attacks make its future very uncertain. I do not know what will happen to Kurdistan or to my people in the future. We want to be in charge of our own lives and to have the freedom to be Kurdish without fear. For this to happen, we are going to need the help of the countries in the West. In some countries, people have already set up groups to demonstrate on behalf of the Kurds (see opposite).

   Until we have freedom, the fighting will continue and thousands more people will be killed. I feel very lucky to be in this country and away from the fighting. I miss my friends, though, and I worry about whether they are safe. I am getting used to my new life now. But I still hope that one day I will be able to go back home, to Kurdistan.

Goodbye!

FACT FILE

1918 – Collapse of Ottoman Empire.

1920 – Treaty of Sevres sets up plans for an independent Kurdish state, but these are later ignored when Turkey refuses to cooperate.

1923 – Sheikh Mahmoud declares himself 'King of Kurdistan' in Suleymaniyah (Iraq). The British suppress this movement and force the Sheikh to go into exile in India.

1923 – Treaty of Lausanne ignores Kurdish calls for independence.

1925 – Sheikh Said leads an unsuccessful uprising in Turkey. South Kurdistan is incorporated in the new Iraqi state under a British mandate (control). A new border divides the Kurds in Iraq and Turkey.

1930 – Rebellion in Mt Ararat crushed by Turkey with Iranian help.

1937-8 – Kurdish uprising in Dersim, Turkey.

1943-5 – Kurdish revolt in Iraq led by Mustafa Barzani.

1946-7 – First Kurdish Republic founded in Mahabad, Iran.

1970 – Kurds and Iraqis sign an agreement giving the Kurds self-rule.

1975 – Algiers agreement ends Iranian support for Iraqi Kurds. Kurdish resistance collapses.

1979 – Following overthrow of Iranian Shah (king), Kurds gain freedom in Iranian Kurdistan. Crushed by the new Iranian leader, Ayatollah Khomeini, in 1980.

1984 – Kurdistan Workers Party (PKK) launches armed struggle (guerilla war) against the Turkish government.

1988 – Saddam Hussein orders the bombing of the Kurdish town of Halabja, killing 5,000 people with chemical weapons. This is part of a campaign which killed 180,000 people.

1991 – Kurds briefly liberate Iraqi Kurdistan after the Gulf War but are then forced to flee to the mountains and across the Turkish and Iranian borders. The United Nations sets up safe havens (known as 'Free Kurdistan') after Kurdish children are seen dying on TV screens in the West.

1994 – Turkey steps up the war against the PKK. This time Kurds flee from Turkey to Iraq. Economic restrictions continue to create hardship in Iraqi Kurdistan. Iran continues to bomb 'Free Kurdistan'.

INDEX

Photocredits
All the pictures in this book were supplied by Frank Spooner Pictures apart from the following pages: cover inset, 3, 29: Roger Vlitos; cover, title page, 6, 15 top, 19 bottom right: Andrew Penny; 5: Panos Pictures; 11 bottom, 20: Eye Ubiquitous.